# The Ice Journey

## by Grandma Valerie

*Valerie*

Hello, I am Grandma Valerie. I live in Wales. If you look on a globe, or map of the world, you will see that Great Britain is just north of France.

Look closely and you will see that The British Isles are actually four small countries. England, Scotland, Ireland, and right in the middle is Wales.

Gradually the four Kingdoms were united. That is why Britain is called Great Britain or the United Kingdom. Just like the other countries in Europe, each country has its own history, culture and traditions.

The British Isles are part of Europe, where there are lots of countries and people speaking many different languages.

They are all Europeans and their descendants have spread out all around the world.

It is difficult to find out about our earliest ancestors because most of their exciting adventures happened so long ago. Long before people wrote the stories down.

We have to be detectives and, from the clues they left behind, work out what might have happened.

Now it's time to settle down and listen to an amazing story. A story about the very difficult and dangerous journeys that people made as the last great Ice Age came to an end. It's also the story of some scientists who have been very clever detectives; they believe they have found enough clues to show that about 17,000 years ago, a few people could have travelled from south-western France, all the way across the Atlantic Ocean, to America.

Until very recently all the scientists were agreed that the first people to arrive in America had come from Asia. That they had walked over a land bridge that used to exist between part of the Russian Federation and Alaska, one of the United States of America – an incredible journey! Later on more ice from the last great Ice Age melted and the sea covered that land bridge. It is now called The Bering Strait.

In 1933 some Stone Age tools were found at a place called Clovis in New Mexico, U.S.A. The scientists were able to date the tools because they were found next to some Mammoth bones.

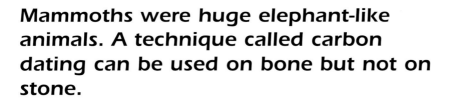

Mammoths were huge elephant-like animals. A technique called carbon dating can be used on bone but not on stone.

They dated the bones to about 11,000 years ago. Perfect for the theory that the first people in America had come from Asia.

Before that the land bridge between Asia and America had been buried under the ice cap of the last great Ice Age.

Archaeologists thought that there was no point in digging deeper because no people could have lived in America earlier than about 11,500 years ago.

But then an archaeologist did dig deeper, at a site near Pittsburgh, Pennsylvania, one of the eastern States of America, and found some stone tools from an even earlier date.

Where had they come from?

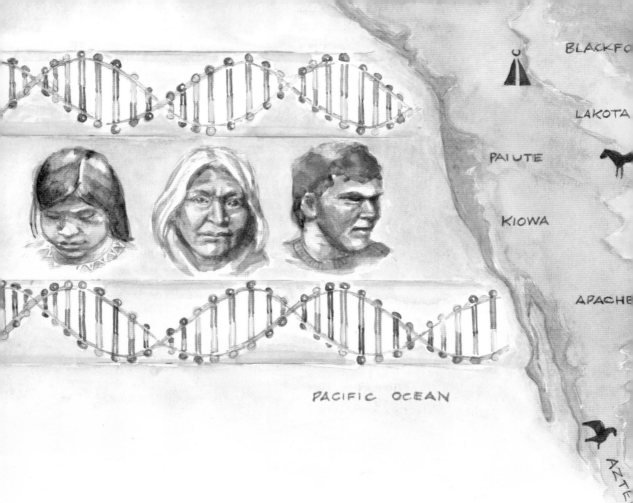

A scientist, who studied genetics, has been able to prove that most Native Americans share the same genetic material, called DNA, as people in Asia. A good clue supporting the theory that, as the last great Ice Age was coming to an end, people had crossed over the land bridge from Asia to Alaska.

But on the eastern side of America the DNA research was not as clear. Many scientists now think that people had been arriving in America, in small numbers, for thousands of years – perhaps as long ago as 30,000 years.

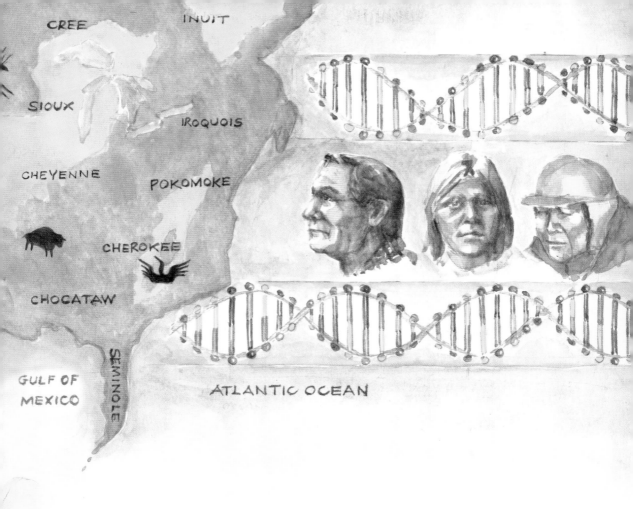

30,000 years ago the land bridge was deep under the ice. Travel from Asia would have been very, very difficult. Most hunter-gatherers follow herds of grazing animals, horses and reindeer. These only go where there is food to eat and no fodder grows on ice. Another curious thing was that these earlier tools were being found on the eastern side of America, nearer to Europe. Tools that are very similar to those being made in Europe and no tools like these have been found in Asia. In 2002 a scientist identified DNA that could have come from Europe about 15,000 years ago in Native Americans who live near the great lakes in America.

Thousands of miles away, on the other side of the Atlantic Ocean, in south-western France a group of people, called the Solutreans, lived by the sea. They were very clever toolmakers making tools from wood, bone and stone. Only the stone tools have survived from so long ago and these are very similar to those found on the eastern side of America.

A few archaeologists began to wonder, could this just be a coincidence?

Could some Solutrean people really have made an incredible journey across the Atlantic Ocean?

They thought it was impossible but they asked some Eskimos what they thought. Eskimos are one of the Inuit tribes who live in Alaska and northern Canada. They are some of the last hunter-gatherer peoples on earth. Until only just over a hundred years ago their lives would have been very similar to that of the Solutrean people. Although nowadays summers in south-western France are long and warm and winters short and mild 17,000 years ago, at the end of the last great Ice Age, it was very, very cold, an arctic region, very like Alaska today.

Today the Inuit peoples live modern lives with cars and supermarkets but some are very interested in their ancient crafts and ancient way of life. Some still make traditional sealskin clothing, using seal bone needles, just like one in a museum in France and that is over 20,000 years old!

Some Inuit fisherman still use traditionally made boats. They say that these flexible boats are safer in icy waters than modern boats.

A fisherman explained that to an Eskimo ice is land. At the end of the last great Ice Age, even as far south as south-western France, the Atlantic Ocean would have been full of ice floes forming a sort of ice-bridge. He thought the Solutrean people could have done it! They would have pulled their boats on to ice floes at night, just as he does, and survived such a long, amazing and dangerous journey.

In modern times a few people have rowed small boats across the Atlantic Ocean.

Thousands of years before scientists thought that people could have lived in America a Solutrean man; let's call him "Ia", the Welsh word for ice, gazed out to sea.

He was trying to work out what to do for the best. His family was cold and hungry.

As it got colder people would
have moved south to get away from
the cold. Some might have settled in
south-western France and perhaps they
told their children about land to the north.

In the time that Ia lived most people probably thought that tales of lands in the north were just folk stories but Ia began to wonder if the stories could be true. He and his friends talked about it all through the long dark winter, could there really be land to the north beyond the ice and snow?

When spring came, Ia, Taith, and some of their friends, decided to go and look for a new home where they hoped there would be plenty to eat.

Today we know that the folk tales were true. There is land to the north, but Ia would never find it as it was still buried deep under the ice. We know that there is no land between Europe and America but Ia did not know this. They didn't have a map! They did not know that they would have to travel for weeks before they saw land again. We don't know how long it took them in their tiny boats. It was a very dangerous journey across thousands of miles of icy ocean.

Ia, Taith and their friends took their harpoons and lived on the fish and seals they caught on the way. They could have taken dried or smoked fish. Even today, in remote communities, long ropes of fish hung out to dry in the sun and wind is a common sight. Before people learned to freeze, pickle or tin fish, drying and smoking were the only ways to preserve the catch. They could have eaten raw fish. Some people still do, the normal way to eat oysters is to have them raw.

The Solutreans have faded from history but the tools they left behind are good clues and scientists will go on and on looking for more and more evidence to prove that some Solutrean people really did make this amazing journey.

What do you think? It is time for you to be a detective and find out more for yourself.

# Learn with Grandma

An interactive CD-Rom is available from our website: www.4learningenglish.com. The best way to learn any language is to hear it spoken by a native speaker.

Please visit www.4learningenglish.com for a free download of interesting websites with more information about this story.

Find out what these words mean by looking in a dictionary, or ask a grown up, and then use the word in a sentence.

Gradually. Culture. Traditions. Descendants. Detectives. Incredible. Arctic. Genetic. Theory. Data. Technique. Archaeologists. Coincidence. Ancient. Flexible. Exploring. Prehistory. Probably. Harpoons. Remote. Communities. Preserve. Evidence.

# Can you answer these questions?

How can we find out about history before people wrote the history down?

What were the people who lived in south-western France called?

What was the weather like in south-western France 17,000 years ago?

What is the weather like there today?

What did the Solutrean people eat?

What was their most important food source?

Why could they not move to north, east or south?

How did the Ice Age people preserve their fish?

What other ways do we use today to preserve fish?

What is the range of mountains that separate Spain and France called?

Why did the Eskimos think the Solutrean people could have come across the ocean?

What happened to make the sea level rise?

Why did the Inuit fisherman think that a traditional boat was safer?

What year were stone-age tools found in Clovis, New Mexico?

What does a geneticist study?

What clues did the Solutrean people leave in America?

## Things to think and talk about.

Think about all the things the Solutrean people and the Inuit peoples made from sealskins.

Think about why we want to save seals today.

Think about how difficult and dangerous the journeys were that our ancient ancestors made across the Atlantic Ocean and over a land bridge from Asia.

Think of all the different things we eat that come from the sea.

Think about different ways to preserve fish.

## Things to do.

Visit a local museum to see the earliest Stone Age artifacts.

Visit an aquarium, oceanarium or fish market to see different types of fish.

Visit a supermarket and see how many different ways and types of preserved fish you can find.

## An outside game:

Island hopping is fun. Choose places to be 'islands' and run from island to island. You could do this all the way across a park or playground and pretend that you are crossing the Atlantic Ocean. Someone could be a shark and try to catch people off the islands, then those people become sharks too. The winner is the last person left on an island

## Art.

Make a model of an ice age boat.

Paint a picture of Ice Age people who lived by the sea. Grandma Valerie would love to see your paintings.

## Drama.

With your friends or class make up a play about living in arctic conditions.

# Find out more about our world.

Find the Bering Strait.

Find the Atlantic Ocean on a globe or map of the world.

Find New Mexico on a map of America.

Find Ohio on a map of America.

Find Pennsylvania on a map of America.

Find The Pyrenean mountains on a map of Europe.

Please visit www.4learningenglish.com for a free download of interesting geography websites.

# Science.

Will the sea rise if the polar ice caps melt?
Put ice cubes in a glass, add water and mark the level on the glass. After the ice has melted, look at the mark.
What has happened to the level?

People are now worried about global warming. They are right to worry. If the world does get hotter more snow and ice will melt but the ice floating on the sea will not make the sea levels higher. The sea could only rise if all the ice on the land melted and was allowed to flow into the sea. If the earth gets warmer we must do our best to use the water from the mountains wisely - to irrigate more land and provide the extra water people need.

Make an edible DNA model from sweets!
You will need.
2 different coloured long liquorice cords with a soft centre.
A large packet of small soft sweets with four different colours.
A box of cocktail sticks.
Needle & thread.
How to make the model.
Cut the cords into 3cm pieces and, with the needle & thread sew them into two chains of alternating colours. Lay them down so that the same colours are opposite each other.
Put two different coloured soft sweets on each cocktail stick and make a ladder with the chains. Twist the chains for the double helix pattern.
For full instructions, with colour pictures and scientific explanation, go to www.4learningenglish.com

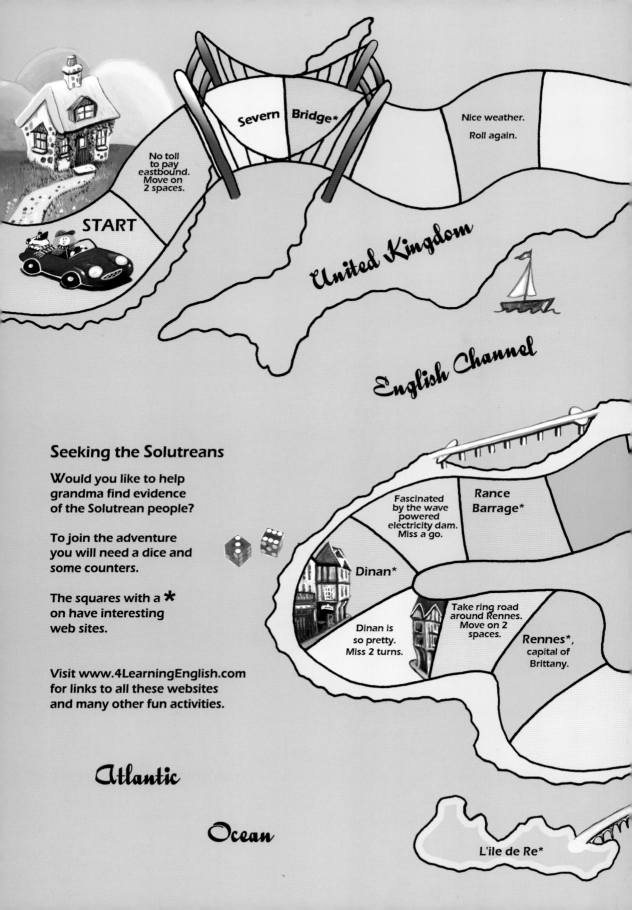

Severn Bridge*

Nice weather.
Roll again.

No toll
to pay
eastbound.
Move on
2 spaces.

START

United Kingdom

English Channel

## Seeking the Solutreans

Would you like to help
grandma find evidence
of the Solutrean people?

To join the adventure
you will need a dice and
some counters.

The squares with a *
on have interesting
web sites.

Visit www.4LearningEnglish.com
for links to all these websites
and many other fun activities.

Fascinated
by the wave
powered
electricity dam.
Miss a go.

Rance
Barrage*

Dinan*

Dinan is
so pretty.
Miss 2 turns.

Take ring road
around Rennes.
Move on 2
spaces.

Rennes*,
capital of
Brittany.

Atlantic

Ocean

L'ile de Re*